Signature of A Muslim

Junaid Rafique Al Hijazi

amana publications

First Edition
(1431AH/2010AC)

amana publications
10710 Tucker Street
Beltsville, Maryland 20705-2223 USA
Tel: (301) 595-5999 / Fax: (301) 595-5888
E-mail: amana@igprinting.com
Website: www.amana-publications.com

Library of Congress Cataloging-in-Publication Data

Al Hijazi, Junaid Rafique, 1976-
Signature of a Muslim / Junaid Rafique Al Hijazi.
p. cm.
ISBN 978-1-59008-061-0
1. Da'wah (Islam) 2. Islam--Relations. 3. Islam. I. Title.
BP170.85.A433 2010
297.7'4--dc22

2010018690

Printed in Turkey By Mega Print

Table of Contents

بسم الله الرحمن الرحيم

الصلوة والسلام عليك يا رسول الله ﷺ

"For Allah hath sent down to you (Oh Muhammad) the Book and wisdom and taught you that which you previously did not know."

(Qur'an, 4: 113)

Introduction

THE PURPOSE OF THIS BOOK is twofold: firstly to help us understand the necessary components that we personally need to be effective in giving *da'wa* (inviting people to Islam, the worship of Allah, and the belief in the Prophet Muhammad *sall-Allahu alayhi wa sallam*), and secondly to introduce some concepts to help us achieve better results. The two parts of the book should give you an insight into the world of *da'wa* in today's material, pretentious and dangerous world where misguidance and *fitna* (mischief) are king.

In an age where the *ummah* (the Muslim community) is disjointed, leaderless, and without true role models, I still believe that in our own way we all have the potential to be role models and leaders.

The questions that should arise when reading this book are simple but incredibly important. For example, am I a believer? What or who matters to me the most? Which parts of my character can I change? What is my legacy? Can I exert more influence to change others around me?

Answering some of these questions takes courage because it means performing a self- analysis and addressing our weaknesses. Ultimately, our egos will tell us that we are important and that we don't need to change. However, how important are we? If we take a timescale and look at how many came before us and how many will come after us, in the end many of us will just whither away in the thoughts and minds of only a few people who knew us, and we will eventually fade away into oblivion. This book will help address the questions raised above so that you are in a position to decide for yourself what legacy you want to leave behind, and even if the book can help you to change one person, that in itself is a great achievement.

The beauty of understanding your own potential, the issue with which the first part of the book deals, is that there is no limit to what you can achieve in effecting personal internal change and then impacting others positively. Thus, part one of the book will show you where you are in terms of your personal development, and part two will equip you with new tools for giving *da'wa* that are very often over looked.

Part two is a window to the world of an unspoken language. It is an insight into a universal language that if you can read, understand and reciprocate, it will give you a cutting edge to perform da'wa in a way that will have you speaking to people on a level with which they feel comfortable.

Thus, the book will give you an overall insight into yourself, essential preparatory tools for *da'wa* such as humility and *taqwa* (God consciousness; awe or fear of Allah), as well as concepts that will equip you to achieve better results when calling people to Islam.

Part One

Necessary Elements for giving Da'wa

Am I Believer?

WE CAN ALL MAKE A DIFFERENCE for the good in this world, even if we think we lack the knowledge, wisdom and tools to do so. If we don't have much knowledge, maybe an action someone sees will have an impact on them. If we don't have wisdom, maybe our manners will touch someone's heart. If we lack the tools for *da'wa,* then maybe our sincerity will shine through. We all have a position, and we can all do something to affect change for the good in someone. But knowing where you stand when it comes to your level of belief is important, since it will give you a valuable indication of how much you can do, as well as showing you what your limits are.

If you are a Muslim, I'm sure your answer to the question in the title will be, "Of course I'm a believer."

If so, then ponder over this:

"Oh you who believe, believe" (Qur'an, 4:136)

The verse tells us that there are levels of belief, and this is proven by the hadith where the Prophet, *sall-Allahu alayhi wa sallam* (may Allah bless him and grant him peace), said, *"Whenever you see an evil act, stop it with your hands, and if you are not able to do that, then speak out with your tongue, and if you are not able to do that, hate it in your heart, and that is the lowest form of iman (belief or faith)."* (Muslim)

In assessing what type of belief we have, there are two points that I want to make:

The first point is that how we perceive the Prophet, *sall-Allahu alayhi wa sallam,* is the key.

Please read the following eleven times before continuing:

"Laa illa ha il lallaah Muhammadur rasoo lullah."

(There is no God but Allah; Muhammad is the messenger of God.)

No doubt, we all love Allah, but ask yourself how much you love the Prophet, *sall-Allahu alayhi wa sallam.* Loving him is not tantamount to shirk (worshipping something other than Allah and/or giving partners to Allah) since love does not equate to worship. There is also no such thing as loving him too much, as long as you know that he is the Messenger of God.

On one occasion, a man asked the Prophet, *sall-Allahu alayhi wa s allam: "When is the hour?" He replied, "What have you prepared for it?" The man said, "Nothing, except that I love Allah and His Messenger." The Prophet, sall-Allahu alayhi wa sallam, said, "You will be with those whom you love."* (Bukhari and Muslim)

This is a beautiful hadith that probably brings great relief to many people, but for some it raises the questions of whether they really love the Prophet, *sall-Allahu alayhi wa sallam*, and how much they love him. While I do not doubt that many of you know a lot about him, there are some who don't. After all, how can you love someone you know nothing about? Ask yourself what you love about the Prophet, *sall-Allahu alayhi wa sallam,* and if you can't answer the question, then find something. It can be anything, but let it be something important to you and your life. I remember speaking to an English lady who provided foster care for abandoned cats, and I was shocked when she related the story of when the Prophet, *sall-Allahu alayhi wa sallam*, cut around his garment so he would not awaken a cat that had fallen asleep next to him.

As per our actions, when you love someone, you talk about him or her. You aspire to be like him or her. I'm not asking you to follow every single *sunnah* (the customary practice of Prophet Muhammad, *sall-Allahu alayhi wa sallam*) there is because that would be impossible. I'm not even asking you to follow most of them. However, if you are not following any, try to find some that are easy for you to follow and introduce them into your lives. I once wanted to give something to my wife for our home. I bought some leather table mats after remembering that the Prophet, *sall-Allahu alayhi wa sallam*, would have his meal set out on leather. In that way, my table looked trendy; my wife was happy, and I was following a *sunnah*.

The second point I want to make is that when dealing with the level of your belief, it comes down to assessing your capabilities. How much can you do; how much is needed to make a difference?

Very often, when first practicing our faith, we tend to go a hundred miles an hour, and before long we grind to an abrupt halt. We even worry about going back to what we used to be like.

Sound familiar?

The answer lies in consistency. Even if you can do only a little or even just the obligatory, it is doing it consistently that counts.

Hazrat Aisha, *radiya'llahu 'anha* (may Allah be pleased with her), narrates that once the Prophet came while a woman was sitting with her. He said, "Who is she?" Aisha replied, "She is so and so," and she told him about the woman's (excessive) praying. He said disapprovingly, *"Do (good) deeds that are within your capacity (without being overtaxed), as Allah does not get tired (of giving rewards), but (surely) you will get tired, and the best deed (act of worship) in the sight of Allah is that which is done regularly."* (Bukhari)

One's mindset should be to practice a comfortable level of actions and then to guard them jealously for as long as possible, even if that means only doing the obligatory acts if that is the only means of achieving consistency. Ultimately, only you know how much you can do.

Jaber bin Abdullah Al-Ansari, *radiya'llahu 'anhu* (may Allah be pleased with him) narrated that a man asked the Messenger of Allah, "Do you think that if I perform the obligatory prayers, fast in Ramadan (the ninth month in the Islamic lunar calendar; the month in which Muslims fast from dawn to dusk), treat as lawful that which is lawful and treat as forbidden that which is forbidden, and do nothing further, I shall enter Paradise?" He responded, "Yes." (Muslim)

The above should give you an indication of what level of belief you have. So ask yourself this: Am I a believer? What do I love about the Prophet, *sall-Allahu alayhi wa sallam;* which *sunnah* is easy for me to follow? Am I performing my religion consistently?

This assessment will now give you the platform for knowing how much and what type of *da'wa* you can give. If you feel that you have little belief, then you can give *da'wa* according to your own comfortable level. If you feel that you have a strong level of belief, then your options are many. Good luck!

Perception or Deception?

"Nor are the living the same as those who are dead"
(Qur'an, 35:22)

ONE THING I'VE NOTICED IS THAT the mindset of Muslims is not aligned with our belief system. It's like having a Renault Clio engine in a Phantom Rolls Royce. While you might be thinking that's a silly thing to say, it's not silly when we realize that we have been handed the greatest religion, the greatest book, the greatest prophet, the greatest code of life, and the keys to the afterlife, but we just don't understand our own potential.

I want you to think about the following questions.

How do others perceive me?

How can I use Islam to influence people in today's material world?

How accurate is my own perception of Islam?

How do others perceive me?

We should all consider ourselves to be walking advertising boards. The key is that we want people to think we have a good character because of our faith, and that should be our advertising campaign. "Look at my impeccable character. I am a Muslim." Instead of bringing about thoughts in our counterparts' minds such as an Arab wielding an AK47 assault rifle on horseback with an RPG attached to the saddle, spending some time with you should bring out in people some beautiful feelings. The way we feel often influences our views. If you can make someone feel good, and if they know that your character is because you are Muslim, they may have a totally different view about Islam.

Since the topic is perception, and no, it isn't enough to have a beard or to wear a *hijab* (scarf) while walking around angrily, staring at the infidels and hoping they would all die. It's about our *adab* (manners and etiquette) around others. The Prophet, *sall-Allahu alayhi wa sallam*, changed people with his manners. He spoke to his enemies like he spoke to his companions. If he hadn't, who would have changed?

Please note here that it is not how many people you successfully change but the amount of influence you can exert and the effort you give. Remember that some prophets will be raised on the Final Day with only a handful of followers, and they were prophets. Furthermore, Nuh, *'alayhi's-salam* (peace be upon him), gave *da'wa* for approximately one thousand years.

Since Rome wasn't built in a day, here are some narrations and actions that can get you started on your advertising campaign. Choose some you find easy to practice, or choose your own. As a rule of thumb, the hardest to perform are usually the most effective.

'Amr Ibn Al-'Aas, *radiya'llahu 'anhu,* said:

> *"The Messenger of Allah, sall-Allahu alayhi wa sallam, upon meeting the worst of people, would face them while speaking to them and thus bring about their affection. He would face and speak to me until I thought I was from the best of people, so I asked him: 'Oh Messenger of Allah, am I better or Abu Bakr?' He said: 'Abu Bakr.' So I said: 'Oh Messenger of Allah, am I better or 'Umar?' He replied: "Umar.' So I said: 'Oh Messenger of Allah, am I better or 'Uthmaan?' He said: "Uthmaan.' When I asked the Messenger of Allah and he told me, I wished that I had never asked him." (At-Tirmidhi and Muslim – hasan (good, excellent, a hadith that is reliable but that is not sahih (healthy, sound, with no defects, a hadith that is authentic and at the highest level of reliability).* (Bukhari has a similar narration.)

Furthermore, all accounts of the Prophet's, *sall-Allahu alayhi wa sallam,* conversations tell us that he always waited for the other person to finish speaking before he replied. He would never interrupt them.

While being careful not to seem to be a fake in front of others, it must be remembered that people paint a picture according to first impressions and body language. Making someone feel important brings about warmth, sincerity, friendship, trust, and respect. If you face them and pay them your full attention, it also means you're listening. If you think about it, most good doctors practice this, and it usually acts in a therapeutic way to relieve some anxiety before a cure is proposed.

If you find something said that you dislike, don't rebuke the person, even though that's the easiest option. Just stay quiet or change the topic. If you're ready to hit them in the face, turn your face and body away. Better still, walk away. Don't let your *nafs* (ego) dictate your next move; let the *sunnah* dictate it. Sometimes doing the unexpected is enough to challenge people's perceptions, and it may make them think. Remember Imam (Muslim religious leader) Ghazali became famous after he was pushed into a river for no reason and then asked the person who pushed him to forgive him if he had done something wrong.

> "Once, a person was verbally abusing Abu Bakr, *radiya'llahu 'anhu*, while the Prophet, *sall-Allahu alayhi wa sallam*, was curiously watching with a smile. After taking much abuse quietly, Abu Bakr responded to a few of his comments. At this, the Prophet exhibited his disapproval, got up, and left. Abu Bakr caught up with the Prophet and wondered, 'O Messenger of Allah, he was abusing me, and you remained sitting. When I responded to him, you disapproved and got up.'
>
> "The Messenger of Allah responded, 'There was an angel with you responding to him. When you responded to him, Shaytan took his place.' He then said, 'O Abu Bakr, there are three solid truths: If a person is wronged and he forbears it (without seeking revenge) just for the sake of Allah Almighty, Allah will honor him

and give him the upper hand with His help; if a person opens a door of giving gifts for cementing relationships with relatives, Allah will give him abundance; and if a person opens a door of seeking charity for himself to increase his wealth, Allah will further reduce his wealth.'" (Musnad of Ahmad ibn Hanbal)

A man asked the Prophet, *sall-Allahu alayhi wa sallam*, "What in Islam is the best?" He, *sall-Allahu alayhi wa sallam*, answered, "To feed people and to say salaam (The Islamic greeting of peace) to everyone, whether you know them or not." (Bukhari).

These *sunnahs* have almost been lost. When was the last time you didn't interrupt a person when they were talking? How often do you take the easiest option when insulted and fire back? When did you last face someone completely during some conversation? Do you only greet people you know?

How can I use Islam to influence people in today's materialistic world?

Some of us are chasing large bank balances but are morally bankrupt. Some of us have morals but are lopsided in every other aspect of life, having no desire and drive for success in life. So where does material gain and *dunya* (this world, or worldly life) fit into Islam, or are these things completely shunned?

Remember this *dua* (supplication to Allah): "*Rabba na ataina fid dunya, hassana tunw wa fil akhirati, hassanatuw wa kin azaban nar*" (our Lord, give to us the good of this life, the good of the Hereafter, and protect us from the fire (of Hell)).

What is interesting about this *dua* is that *dunya* is mentioned first. This is because we must live in it and fulfill obligations that will allow us to be successful in the next life. It doesn't mean that we should enjoy this world as much as possible. We should manage our relationships and our worldly obligations in an Islamic way. All this, however, does not negate the fact that *dunya* has its importance and its place that cannot be overlooked.

The importance of this world is also illustrated by the following *hadith*:

Happiness has four elements: a good wife, a spacious house, a good neighbor, and a comfortable riding beast. (Reported by Ibn Hibbaan in his Sahih.)

The Prophet, *sall-Allahu alayhi wa sallam,* often used to pray, "Our Lord, forgive my sins, make my house spacious, and bless me in my sustenance."

Using *dunya* to promote our belief can be quite an easy way to influence people. After all, who says you can't use *dunya* in your advertising campaign and be really creative?

So then, in today's world where most of the *Sunni* (the main body of Muslims) *ulama* (scholars) are still driving Datsuns to their *madaris* (schools), why not use your means and success to influence people? Pulling up to a function in a Range Rover would command a lot more respect in today's world, especially when trying to influence the young. If you think that's being cunning, then what's wrong with being cunning if, for example, it makes a teenager look up to you and ultimately makes him a better person through your guidance? You're not asking him to worship your car; you're not running him over. However, you're using your material possessions to impress someone. Let's face it, in today's world no one listens to a man who pulls up in a Datsun, no matter how good his speech is or how high his trousers are.

I am not asking you to go out and waste money and buy a Bentley for a hundred thousand pounds (which will depreciate by a large amount each year). However, sometimes using what we have at our disposal can become an effective weapon of influence. Since the Prophet, *sall-Allahu alayhi wa sallam*, said that the best charity is that which you spend on your family, if your large, five-bedroom house with a pool room and heated swimming pool means that your family is comfortable and can make people view Islam in a different light, then why not?

HOW ACCURATE IS MY OWN PERCEPTION OF ISLAM?

Happiness has four elements: a good wife, a spacious house, a good neighbor, and a comfortable riding beast. (Ibn Hibbaan)

To understand the third question about our own perception of Islam, let's relate the *hadith* to today's world. I would consider a Range Rover, S Class Mercedes, BMW 7 Series, etc. to be comfortable riding beasts. Likewise, I would consider sitting on heated leather seats an underrated *sunnah* synonymous with the *sunnah* of sitting on a hot-blooded camel or horse. It just proves that the *sunnah* has no sell-by date and is up to date. In fact our minds are not advanced enough to keep up with the Prophet's, *sall-Allahu alayhi wa sallam,* sayings.

Here's another example of how we can change our own and other people's perceptions about the *sunnah.* Again, it proves the world today is backward and is only just catching up.

Imam Zarqani records a *hadith* in his Sharh Mawahibul Luduniya where the Prophet, *sall-Allahu alayhi wa sallam,* said: *"Allah Almighty presented the whole world (earth, universe) to me, and (so) I am looking at it and also everything that is going to take place in the universe, just as I am looking at the palm of my hand."*

Now, when we walk around with our mobile phones in the palm of our hands, can we not access the world through various software applications? Examples of these applications include Facebook, GPS, the internet, the news, and sports, just to mention a few. Ultimately, isn't this information in the palm of our hands? So ask yourself, who's catching up with whom?

The point I want to make is that the *sunnah* is considered a strange thing to some people, and they don't know how to relate to it at times or even how to consider it as a thing that is relevant. The truth of the matter is that the *sunnah* is up to date, not out of date, and will always be up to date no matter in which timeframe the world may be.

Ever wondered why the best heart surgeons are Muslim?

It was narrated by Abbas bin Malik that Malik bin Sa'sa'a said that Allah's Apostle described to them his Night Journey, saying, "While I was lying in Al-Hatim or Al-Hijr, suddenly someone came to me and cut my body open from here to here." I asked Al-Jarud who was by my side, "What does he mean?" He said, "It means from his throat to his pubic area," or said, "From the top of the chest." The Prophet further said, "He then took out my heart. Then a gold tray of belief was brought to me and my heart was washed and was filled (with belief) and then returned to its original place." (Bukhari, Muslim, Tirmidhi, Abu Dawood, Ibn Maja)

It was reported by Anas Bin Malik that the Prophet, *sall-Allahu alayhi wa sallam*, said: *"My heart was extracted and it was washed with the water of Zamzam and then it was restored in its original position, after which it was filled with faith and wisdom."* (Muslim)

Thus, is it a coincidence that the best heart surgeons are Muslim?

On April 12, 1961, Russian-born Yuri Gagarin became the first human to travel to outer space. But was he?

On the 27th of Rajab and one year before *Hijra*, the Prophet, *sall-Allahu alayhi wa sallam*, undertook a miraculous and magical journey where he traveled to the heavens to meet Allah and receive our daily prayers. This is the first known record of space travel and is authenticated by Allah himself in the Qur'an and by various authentic *ahadith*.

"Glory to (Allah) Who did take His servant for a Journey by night from the Sacred Mosque to the farthest Mosque, whose precincts We did bless,- in order that We might show him some of Our Signs: for He is the One Who heareth and seeth (all things)." (Qur'an, 17:1)

It is narrated on the authority of Anas ibn Malik that the Messenger of Allah, *sall-Allahu alayhi wa sallam*, said: "I was brought al-buraq who is an animal white and long, larger than a donkey but smaller than a mule, who would place its hoof at a distance equal to the range of vision. I mounted it and came to *Bait-al Maqdis* (Jerusalem). I then tethered it to the ring used by the prophets. I entered the area of the mosque and prayed two *rak'at* (units of prayer) in it. I then came out and Gabriel brought me a vessel of wine and a vessel of milk. I chose the milk, and Gabriel said, 'You have chosen *al-fitra*, the natural way.' *He then ascended with me into the lower heavens and requested that they be opened."* (The *hadith* continues) (Muslim)

This is proof that, even though we might think that the *sunnah* is not relevant to today's world, we are wrong and that while scientific breakthroughs may be big news for some, they are just old news for the Prophet, *sall-Allahu alayhi wa sallam.* The phrase "been there done that" is an apt one.

CHECKING YOUR *NAFSOMETER*

BEFORE GETTING INTO THIS TOPIC, HERE'S a small exercise for you to do:

Take a piece of paper (or pad) and a pen. Now write down the most shameful things that you have done in your life. Then draft a response to Allah for each one that will be questioned on the Day of Judgment. Never thought about it? Start now!

The question to ask yourself here is, "How can I ask others to remember the Day of Judgment if I don't remember it myself?"

Now that we're ready to enter this topic, ask yourself the following question:

Do people see you as arrogant?

How you are around others decides how much impact you can have on them. In today's world, having humility and controlling pride are the most overlooked, necessary components of being a good Muslim.

Understanding the impact of each one gives us an understanding of our relations with others. For example, when was the last time you heard a person say, "I hate that person; he's so humble." In contrast, how many times have you heard a person say, "I hate that person; he's so arrogant."

The point is that the two cause opposite reactions. Humility attracts, while pride repels. A manager in the workplace who uses his position and authority will be feared but will almost never be respected. A manager who makes his team feel that they are on an equal footing and have the same goals will have a much better chance of commanding loyalty and respect.

In Islam, pride is repulsive, and humility is paramount. False pride was one of the things that Islam came to do away with. It is a shame that now the very same practitioners of that religion are the biggest culprits when it comes to displaying arrogance.

Look at the following verses, which are from the story of Prophet Sulaiman, *'alayhi's-salam*, and the Queen of Sheba:

"He said: 'O chiefs! Which of you can bring me her throne before they come to me surrendering themselves in obedience?'

"An ifrît (a type of jinn) from the jinns said: 'I will bring it to you before you rise from your place (council). And verily, I am indeed strong and trustworthy for such work.'" (Qur'an, Surah 27:38-39)

This *jinn* was ignored purely because of his statement that is underlined. His statement was deemed to be arrogant and was not liked by Sulaiman, *'alayhi's-salam*.

On a separate point, people ask about the beginnings of *tassawuff* (the name given to the practice of spirituality and control of the ego within Sufiism). The Qur'an gives a good indicator of its origins. Referring to his refusal to prostrate to Adam, *'alayhi's-salam*, Allah asked Iblis (Satan):

"Astakbarta, am kunta minal Aleen?" (ARE YOU PROUD, or are you one of the Aleen (the four supreme angels who did not bow?) (Qur'an, 38:75)

Iblis' rise and fall from grace is the greatest example of the destructive nature of pride. He worshipped Allah for thousands of years and was given a position no other *jinn* had obtained. He enjoyed a high status and was in the company of the angels. His pride made him jealous of man; it made him disobey Allah; it made him talk back to his Creator; it made him challenge Allah; it caused him to be cursed and made his home to be the fire of Hell. This one, often conveniently overlooked, flaw made him degrade himself in all these different ways.

On top of this, look at how he further degraded himself. (Arrogant people never accept their faults):

> *"He said: 'Because Thou hast thrown me out of the way, lo! I will lie in wait for them on Thy straight way.'"* (Qur'an, Surah 7:16)

We've dealt with pride; now let's look at humility. Although my following point is slightly off the subject, I've added it in this book to illustrate its importance.

People ask about how they can obtain humility in prayer. Well, essentially, the prayer's components are four: Submission, worship, reverence, and humility. The prayer contains integrals that are demeaning to the ego and humiliating. Look at *sajda* (prostration), for example. For anyone who doubts this statement, next time you go into *sajda*, leave your eyes open, and it will give you a reality check like no other. In *sajda*, what are we actually doing? We are essentially putting the most precious part of our body, which is the face, a part of our body that we spend hours pampering, on the floor. Now, look at this *hadith* in which the Prophet, *sall-Allahu alayhi wa sallam*, said, "The nearest a servant comes to his Lord is when he is prostrating himself, so make supplication (in this state)." (Bukhari). This *hadith* tells us one thing, i.e., that the most humiliating position in our prayer is the most loved by Allah. You may ask why Allah would do this. The answer is simple, because it's the most humble a person can be, and it's the greatest show of submission.

As Muslims, we submit to Allah as slaves, and thus these acts are transformed from acts of humiliation to worship. They elevate us and bring us close to our Creator.

From a *da'wa* point of view, humility serves as a magnificent magnet. If we begin to see ourselves as insignificant and only as slaves, then we can start giving importance to others. This is from where the attraction comes in humility, i.e., the fact that people like to feel important. The concept is similar to getting someone to talk about him or herself. Once he or she gets going, how many times do you find it difficult to then shut him or her up?

The Prophet, *sall-Allahu alayhi wa sallam,* always made people feel that they were the most important to him, and he would thus win their hearts. There is no example of him boasting that he was the Messenger of Allah and behaving in a way where he put himself before others. This was the ultimate attraction.

So the message to you is that if you are not attracting people, then check your ego. No one likes arrogant people. There's no shame in being a slave to your Creator; it's better than being a slave to your ego. Attract people with humility, and use it to your advantage. Good manners and humility are powerful weapons if used correctly.

Since I want to place an element of practicality in this whole book, if you are wondering how you can reduce your pride, then there are some measures that can greatly help. A lot has to do with our mindset.

Look at the following verse:

> *"I have only created jinn and men that they may worship Me."*
> (Qur'an, Surah 51:56)

Now look at this *hadith qudsi* (a *hadith* in which Allah is being quoted). Please note that although this *hadith* has been classified as inauthentic, nearly all commentators agree that its meaning is correct:

> Allah says, "I was a hidden treasure, and I wished to be known, so I created a creation, then made Myself known to them, and they recognized Me."

As human beings, we are all actually extremely vulnerable. To drive home this reality, look at how dependant we are on so many things that we take for granted. For example, if our electricity goes off, we can't cook, watch TV, do our washing, or do our ironing for the next day. In fact, life as we know it just comes to an end! Then look at how many times we encounter death. How many times are we close to having an accident? How often have we been close to or actually had our possessions taken through a burglary or a robbery? How many times have we been in the wrong place at the wrong time? What about many of us who are vulnerable to the elements of nature?

The point is that we are all living on the edge 24 hours a day. You see, arrogance and comfort zones are intrinsically linked. Wondering how? Well, we are arrogant a lot of time when we feel that we are strong and are able to act how we like without accountability and consequence. This is a comfort zone. Allah mentions comfort zones in the Qur'an, and look at what He says:

> *"Hast thou not seen how the ships glide on the sea by Allah's grace, that He may show you of His wonders? Lo! Therein indeed are portents for every steadfast, grateful (heart). And if a wave enshroudeth them like awnings, they cry unto Allah, making their faith pure for Him only. But when He bringeth them safe to land, some of them compromise."* (Qur'an, Surah 31:31-32)

Comfort zones play a massive part in our humility. Even the most ardent atheist becomes a believer when the engines of the aircraft he is on fail! But when he reaches safety again, he goes back to his arrogance.

On the topic of atheists, you often hear atheists saying that religion is a scam and that it's to give hope to poor people. Well, it's funny that poor people will enter Paradise first. It's funny that poor people are almost never in their comfort zone, and maybe that's the reason why they are receiving guidance, i.e., because they are very often the ones with the most humility. How many egotistical rich people do you know, and how many humble poor people do you know? Is it a coincidence?

The word *kaafir* and arrogance are also intrinsically linked. You see, arrogance covers the heart with a wrapping that does not allow any guidance to enter. Humility makes the heart soft and penetrable, allowing knowledge to be obtained, as well as understanding. The word "*kaafir*" means to cover up (from the root word "*kafara*"). Those of us who don't want to admit our helplessness as humans, aren't we just covering it up with our arrogance? Didn't Iblis try to cover up his pride by putting the blame on Allah for misguiding him?

The point I want to make is simple. Our health, our lives, our way of life, and our intellect can all be removed at any time. In the end, we all have to admit to being nothing more than slaves. The first action in our prayer is to raise our hands with our palms facing forward, just like when a person points a gun at us. This means "I submit;" it's a show of humility. It's funny how we submit when we are not in our comfort zone, but become arrogant again if the person puts down the gun!

Dear reader, we all have vulnerable points, and they vary from person to person. These fragile soft spots, if exposed, would leave us high and dry, exposed, and found wanting at any given moment in time. So my advice is don't be in a comfort zone and don't cover up your vulnerable points with arrogance. Be humble, and admit that you are helpless without a higher help and being.

Wondering what all this has to do with *da'wa*? The answer is simple, for Allah to bless your efforts, humility is a must. It brings a person extremely close to Allah and can achieve amazing results in any feat and in any situation. Humility will allow you to be open to accept all people, from all backgrounds and social classes. It will make you versatile, non-judgmental, open minded, approachable, and non-assuming, and all these things will allow you to perform *da'wa* to anyone and everyone. Humility negates a prejudicial selection process and welcomes all with open arms. Humility will allow you to have a mindset that is conducive to accepting anyone for *da'wa* and will allow you to excel in the field.

However, if you have difficulty accepting humility, then my advice to you is to do the following:

Spend the day in a hospital. Next time you are about to bury someone, step inside the grave. Better still, lie in a coffin for a short while. It's not a coincidence that the reward for thinking about death is immense in Islam.

If you are still uncomfortable about being a "*slave*" and with the whole concept of humility, look at how humility has worked for the following individuals, and look at their legacies:

To begin with, consider Prophet Muhammed, *sall-Allahu alayhi wa sallam*:

Anas bin Malik, *radiya'llahu 'anhu,* reported: "A slave-girl of Al-Madinah would take hold of the hand of the Prophet, *sall-Allahu alayhi wa sallam,* and take him wherever she desired."(Bukhari)

It was reported by Aisha, *radiya'llahu 'anha,* that the Prophet, *sall-Allahu alayhi wa sallam,* said: "An angel came to me and said: 'Allâh sends blessings upon you and says: 'If you wish, you may be a Prophet-King or a Slave-Messenger." So Jibrîl, 'alayhi's-salam, indicated to me that I should humble myself, so I said, 'A Prophet-Slave.'" So 'Âishah said: "So after that day, the Prophet, sall-Allahu alayhi wa sallam, never ate while reclining, saying: 'I eat like a slave eats, and I sit like a slave sits.'" (Al Baghawi in his Sharhus Sunnah)

Now take a look at his legacy in one short hadith:

Ibn `Abbas, *radiya'llahu 'anhu,* narrated: "Some people close to the Prophet came and waited for him. When he came out, he approached them and heard them saying: 'What a wonder it is that Allah Almighty and Glorious took one of His creation as His intimate friend – Ibrahim,' while another one said: 'What is more wonderful than His speech to Musa, to whom He spoke directly!' Yet another one said: 'And `Isa is Allah's word and His spirit,' while another one said: 'Adam was chosen by Allah.' The Prophet said: 'I heard your words, and everything you said is indeed true, and I myself am the beloved of Allah (habibullah), and I say this without pride, and I carry the flag of glory on the Day of Judgment and am the first intercessor and the first whose intercession is accepted and the first to stir the circles of Paradise so that Allah will open it for me, and I shall enter it together with the poor among my community, and I say this without pride. I am the most honored of the First and the Last, and I say this without pride.'" (Tirmidhi)

Consider Hazrat Umar, *radiya'llahu 'anhu,:*

Once he was seen running around looking for some camels. He was asked why he didn't order his slaves to look for them. His reply was,

"Who is a bigger slave than me?"

Hazrat Umar was the second caliph of Islam, and the most beloved of companions after Abu Bakr Siddiq. Islam spread far and wide under his caliphate. Although he had a vast amount of wealth at his disposal through this expansion, he would often be seen sleeping on the steps of the mosque, sometimes using a brick for a pillow. When some important people came to visit the king of Islam, when they were introduced to this man sleeping on the steps to the mosque, they exclaimed "This is your king?"

His achievements as the leader of the Muslims are numerous, and his qualities are such that the Prophet said about him that if there were to be another prophet after him, it would be Umar, *radiya'llahu 'anhu.*

Also consider Imam Abu Hanifa, may God have mercy on his soul.

On the subject of humility, he was once slapped by an enemy to whom the Imam replied, "I could slap you in the manner that you have slapped me, but I will not do so. I could complain and report you to the caliph, but I will not do so. I could pray against you at the time of *tahajjud* (a supplementary prayer offered during the night), but I will not do so. I could ask for justice on the Day of Judgment, but I will not do so. I assure you that if I receive my record in my right hand and my intercession is accepted, I will not enter Paradise without you."

He was given the title "The father of *Fiqh*" (Islamic jurisprudence) by the great Imam Shafi'i. When writing his biography, Imam Dhahabi said, "I wrote a volume for each of the imams, but when it came to Abu Hanifa, I realized that one would not be enough and that I needed two." His intellect was legendary. His *taqwa* earned him the title of "The Peg" for his standing in prayer throughout the nights, and he is one of few personalities who recited the whole Qur'an in one *rak'at* (a single unit of the Islamic prayer, consisting of standing, one bowing, two prostrations, and one or two sittings) during his night prayers.

By no means is it an exaggeration to state that it is because of Imam

Abu Hanifa that we understand how to perform *wudhu* (ritual ablution by washing), how to worship, how to perform *hajj* (the ritual pilgrimage to Makkah), how to fast, how to pay the *zakat* (obligatory charity from one's economic surplus and agricultural income), how to trade, how to perform *jumma'a* (the Friday congregational prayer), how to divide our will, how to eat that which is acceptable, along with thousands upon thousands of other important things that affect our daily lives as Muslims. His following has been, is, and continues to be the largest of all in any one era on the planet among the *ummah*.

In all three of the above cases, humility played a crucial role in cementing their legacies and attracting a huge following.

In sum, pride is a repellent, and the attraction of humility serves as a magnet. Oh reader, be attractive, and adopt humility. Beauty and attraction don't only have to be skin deep; Islam allows us to beautify our hearts and souls through our character, so let's start dressing our characters with humility.

Patience

Take a pen and paper. Write down all your difficulties on one side of the page. Then write down the difficulties of the Prophet, *sall-Allahu alayhi wa sallam*, on the other side.

I wanted to include this section on patience as it is so important that it makes up such a large part of a person's life. Oh reader, all influential people who want to impact others positively should know the Islamic definition of patience. This section will do just that, and it will also give us a practical way to deal with it. I also want to give some hope to those people who want to understand why so many things keep going wrong in their lives. Please remember that a person who doesn't adopt patience will undoubtedly be unstable, and no one will take advice from an unstable person.

Here's what Allah tells us about patience:

> *"Oh you who believe! Seek help with patient perseverance and prayer, for Allah is with those who patiently persevere."* (Qur'an, 2:153)
>
> *"Oh you who believe! Persevere in patience and constancy. Vie in such perseverance, strengthen each other, and be pious, that you may prosper."* (Qur'an, 3:200)
>
> *"Patiently, then, persevere - for the Promise of Allah is true, and ask forgiveness for your faults, and celebrate the praises of your Lord in the evening and in the morning."* (Qur'an, 40:55)

In Islam, patience refers to our ability to take suffering and NOT OUR ABILITY TO WAIT FOR A TRAIN AT THE PLATFORM WITHOUT CURSING! It is an essential tool in winning even the most ardent of enemies and is one of the hardest tests to endure. Its success lies in our acceptance of it, in our behavior while being tested, in our ability to endure the test, and in the lasting effects of trials on our characters.

The ability to endure suffering is so important that in nearly every Qur'anic verse on the subject, it is placed before piety, worship and seeking forgiveness, as seen in the verses stated above.

When a Bedouin came to the Prophet, *sall-Allahu alayhi wa sallam,* and asked him a series of questions, one of the issues posed was, "I would like to be the richest man in the world." The Prophet, *sall-Allahu alayhi wa sallam*, said, "Be happy with what you have, and you will be the richest man in the world." (Musnad of Ahmad ibn Hanbal)

Ask yourself when was the last time you were happy to go through a really difficult patch? Please remember that how you react is an indicator of your overall character. In some people, difficulty brings out the evil in them, and in others it softens their hearts.

Since this book is about possessing the character to influence people and about questioning yourself, if you are not happy with what Allah decrees, then your ability to endure suffering is affected. Ultimately, it decides whether Allah is with you or not. After all, how can we affect change in anyone if Allah is not on our side? As the Qur'an reminds us,

"Allah is with those who patiently persevere." (Qur'an, Surah 2:153)

In summary, difficulty should not impact your character negatively. Be happy with whatever is thrown your way, weather the storm patiently, and don't allow the evil in you to raise its head, and you will go from being a good person to being a great person.

For those who think this may be biting off more than you can chew, try it. Be happy with everything Allah decrees, and see how it puts the mind at ease. Then remember what the Qur'an tells us: "Veril*y, with every difficulty there is relief.*" (Qur'an, Surah 94.5)

For those of us who want to know why bad things keep happening to them, lets look at some traditions from the Prophet, *sall-Allahu alayhi wa sallam.* Hopefully it may inspire you to look at difficulty in a different light:

> Narrated Abu Huraira, *radiya'llahu 'anhu:* "Allah's Messenger said, 'If Allah wants to do good to somebody, He afflicts him with trials.'" (Bukhari)

Have you ever considered that Allah might actually love you, hence the trials. The Prophet, *sall-Allahu alayhi wa sallam*, suffered throughout his life, and wasn't he the closest to Allah? In my early years, I once asked a wise scholar about why I was being continuously tested with difficulty. He replied, "Whether you pass or fail is not important; at least you're being tested."

Narrated Abu Sa'id Al-Khudri, *radiya'llahu 'anhu,* and Abu Huraira, *radiya'llahu 'anhu*: "The Prophet said, 'No fatigue, nor disease, nor sorrow, nor sadness, nor hurt, nor distress befalls a Muslim, even if it were the prick he receives from a thorn, but that Allah expiates some of his sins for that.'" (Bukhari)

Look at all these states of being. Both physical and mental pain is included in this *hadith*. The *hadith* more or less includes every kind of ailment we can go through. *Subhan Allah* (glorified is Allah), for each type there is mercy!

So reader, patience is a part of life and our iman. How we deal with it depends on our own perception of why it is happening (the above *hadith*), what is the best response to it (be happy with what is decreed), and where it can lead us (going from good to great).

Still not happy? Take a look at the exercise you did at the beginning of this topic.

Want to be great? Start looking at trials in a different light.

The Role of *Taqwa*

SOME YEARS BACK, I ASKED AN *alim* (Islamic scholar) why a certain individual regularly received visitations from the Prophet, *sall-Allahu alayhi wa sallam*, in her dreams. The answer he gave me was that she had a very deep level of *taqwa* and didn't waste her time playing Play Station. As another *alim* aptly put it, more "pray station" and less Play Station!

Undoubtedly, the role of *taqwa* is tantamount to giving effective *da'wa* and is the magic ingredient to obtaining success.

So what is *taqwa*?

The root word for *taqwa* is "*wa ' ka' ya*" which means to protect. The simplest definition of *taqwa* is that it is to be God conscious, to be aware of Allah and to fear Him. It has connotations of wariness, to be protective of and to be fearful of and can be increased or decreased depending on our level of belief and actions.

Taqwa should be a major concern for all of us. Most of us wonder why certain friendships broke down, why arguments with some people ensued and turned into hatred, why some friends didn't reciprocate the same level of friendship back, why a person wasn't what they seemed from the outset. The answers to all these questions are linked to the plain fact that all relationships should be based on taqwa, and if they are not, they run the risk of early termination, hurtful outcomes and even devastating consequences due to friends turning into enemies. Those relationships that are based on *taqwa* are the strongest and last the test of time. They are stable, rewarding and full of blessing. In fact, the rewards may be greater than we can imagine because when *taqwa* is the focus for all interaction and dictates everything you do then you have a chain reaction as set out below. The key points in this chain reaction are underlined.

The Prophet, *sall-Allahu alayhi wa sallam*, said, "You follow the religion of your friend so choose carefully who you consider to be your friend." (Abu Dawood).

Allah says: *"If you had spent all that is in the earth, you could not have united their hearts, but Allâh has united them. Certainly He is All-Mighty, All-Wise."* (Qur'an, 8:63).

In a *hadith qudsi*, Allah says, *"I am as My servant thinks of Me. I am with him when he remembers Me. If he mentions Me within himself, I mention him within Myself. If he mentions Me in an assembly, I mention him in a better assembly. If he comes near to Me a hand-span, I come near to him the distance of a cubit. If he comes near to Me the distance of a cubit, I come near to him the distance of two outspread arms. If he comes to Me walking, I come to him running."* (Bukhari and Muslim)

The Prophet, *sall-Allahu alayhi wa sallam,* said, *"Allah has decided that it is incumbent on me to bestow my love on those who love one another for my sake, meet one another for my sake and spend on one another for my sake."* (Malik)

Allah says: *"Verily, then Allah loves those who are al-Muttaqun (mindful of Him)."* (Qur'an, 3:76)

The Prophet, *sall-Allahu alayhi wa sallam,* said, *"When Allah loves a slave, he calls out Jibril and says: 'I love so-and-so; so love him.' Then Jibril loves him. After that, he (Jibril) announces to the inhabitants of heavens that Allah loves so-and-so, so love him, and the inhabitants of the heavens (the angels) also love him and then make people on earth love him."* (Bukhari and Muslim)

The Messenger of Allah, *sall-Allahu alayhi wa sallam,* said, *"Allah Almighty has stated, 'I have declared war on anyone who shows enmity to a friend of Mine. My slave does not draw near to Me with anything I love more than what I have made obligatory on him. And my slave continues to draw near to Me with superogatory actions until I love him. When I love him, I become his hearing with which he hears, his seeing with which he sees, his hand with which he strikes, and his foot with which he walks. If he were to ask Me for something, I would give it to him. If he were to ask Me for refuge, I would give him refuge.'"* (Bukhari)

So let's look at this. The chain reaction in itself is mind blowing. It brings together verses and *hadith* that we all know and have seen probably a million times but have overlooked in the context of the subject at hand in this book. The main driving force in all the above is *taqwa*.

The Chain Reaction

1. You choose friendship on the grounds of *taqwa*.
2. The *taqwa* creates a bond that is greater than any other.
3. You meet and mention Allah.
4. Allah mentions you to a superior gathering.
5. This meeting makes it incumbent on Allah to love you.
6. Allah orders Jibril, *alayhi's-salam,* to love you, and Jibril is the greatest of all angels.
7. This leads every inhabitant of the heavens to love you.
8. From this, all those on earth are made to love you.
9. Superogatory actions that are a result of *taqwa* lead to friendship with Allah to such an extent that everything you do and say is sanctioned by Allah Himself, and whatever you ask for is granted.

At this point you may be wondering about certain friendships that you have that are not *taqwa* based. Please remember that sometimes a simple sincere "intention tweak" is all that is required if you are looking at your own relationships and questioning them. For example, what about people at work? What about clients who are crucial to your profession? As I said, "intention tweak" and that is to just remember why you need these relationships in the first place. Working for a living carries its own reward and weight in Islam and is a form of worship in itself. So next time you question why you are with someone during a client meeting, just think, "My intention is to earn a living for Allah's sake."

Furthermore, actions that are not normally for the purposes of *taqwa* can be transformed using this tweak also. The beauty of this is that something as simple as checking your intention can earn you huge "airmiles," as the phrase would have it.

Please note, this does not apply to reading "*Bismallah*" (in the name of Allah) before eating a McDonald's Big Mac somewhere in London.

Since *taqwa* is a spiritual state that is linked to actions, I have compiled a "*taqwa* checklist" that you can use to gain, strengthen and manage your *taqwa*. It is interesting to note that the hardest actions to perform have a bigger impact on *taqwa*. However, please do what is easy and comfortable for you, as consistency is important.

The role of *taqwa* in giving *da'wa* is so important that it cannot be overlooked. I have already shown you what results from *taqwa* above, but in order to be effective in the field one must have a level of *taqwa* that can be seen and quantified. Thus, actions are a must and will prepare and train you so that your *taqwa* will become apparent and visible to all those who come into contact with you. After all, if your *taqwa* is visible, you become a living example of the Qur'an and *sunnah* and not just a zombie with his arms outstretched going about aimlessly with the sole intention of fulfilling the lust for sustenance. Asterisks mark those actions that are particularly potent.

Taqwa Checklist:

1. Never neglect the 5 daily prayers. Establish them, and guard them with jealousy. * * * * *

2. Congregational prayer. * * * * *

3. Choose *sunnahs* that are comfortable for you; guard them, and be constant in performing them.

4. Check your intention constantly

5. Fast as much as you can. * * * * *

6. Cultivate the habit of silence (not when giving *da'wa*)!

7. Love and hate for Allah's sake only
8. Do not harm people with your tongue or actions. * * * * *
9. Be dutiful to your parents. * * * * *
10. Keep ties of kinship.
11. Make *zikr* (remembrance of God) as much as possible. * * * * *
12. Send salutations on the Prophet, *sall-Allahu alayhi wa sallam*. * * * * *
13. Repent regularly. * * * * *
14. Do not delay repentance if you sin. * * * * *
15. Cover a sin with a good deed quickly.
16. Avoid all major sins. * * * * *
17. Speak the truth.
18. Return to the rightful owner what is not yours if entrusted with something.
19. Always be in the state of ablution.
20. Read Qur'an regularly. * * * * *
21. Know and implement the legal obligations that are incumbent on you for your daily life, such as how to perform ablution, how to pray, etc.
22. Establish the night prayer, and guard it. * * * * *

Thus, actions and *taqwa* are linked. But there is yet another link that is often neglected, and that is the link between knowledge and *taqwa*. There is a strong connection between *taqwa* and knowledge, which needs to be realized by us all. It is the key to hidden knowledge and open knowledge and will open a window of opportunity for us that cannot be opened without it. The link between *taqwa* and knowledge is explained as follows by Allah himself:

> *"This is the Book; in it is guidance without doubt, for those with taqwa."* (Qur'an, 2:2)

Thus the Qur'an is only a book of guidance for us if we have *taqwa.* It is true that building, maintaining and growing *taqwa* via actions is an important step. But only when you have *taqwa* can you then gain the knowledge to propagate Islam, as Allah is clearly telling us. Even more importantly, guidance can only come if you understand the knowledge you are gaining, and this is where *taqwa* is essential. In other words, we can deduce from the verse that no *taqwa* means no understanding of knowledge, and no understanding of knowledge means inability to guide others.

On top of this, the world at present is so far away from the truth that the verse is an apt one. We are currently in a world where *haram* (unlawful) is rife, temptation is at a level never previously seen or experienced and where dangerous people control dangerous apparatus that shape how we live. We are constantly in danger, walking a minefield full of trip wires and ambushes, and at each corner our iman is at stake or being tested. This is exactly the reason why we need *taqwa,* and this is exactly the reason why we need *da'wa,* and this is exactly the reason why guarding, training and managing our *taqwa* is paramount. We are in a race, some of us in a race to do good, some of us in a race to do evil. We are all on a race track littered with hurdles that we try to jump. The problem lies in the hurdles being appealingly decorated or even camouflaged by some people in this world who cunningly try to give them an appearance of something else. As Muslims, it is *taqwa* that will illuminate the racetrack and show us the hurdles for what they really are. As for those who wish to camouflage or hide the hurdles, this is the ultimate deception - that freedom to gamble is good, that the freedom to insult our parents is our right, that the freedom to insult people's beliefs is okay, that the freedom to marry the same gender is now acceptable and that the freedom to undress women is civilized. All of this is glossed up by mechanisms of the "free world," that is, the media machine, the glamour media machine, the cinema industry and the TV moguls. May Allah help us.

As the Prophet, *sall-Allahu alayhi wa sallam*, said, "*No, enjoin one another to do what is good, and forbid one another to do what is evil. But when you see niggardliness being obeyed, passion being followed, worldly interests being preferred, everyone being charmed with his opinion, then care for yourself, and leave alone what people in general are doing; for ahead of you are days that will require endurance, in which showing endurance will be like grasping live coals. The one who acts rightly during that period will have the reward of fifty men who act as he does.*" (Abu Dawood).

The *hadith* shows a picture of today's world where holding onto our *taqwa* is more important than it's ever been, where *da'wa* is even more necessary than ever before and where guarding our *iman* is a responsibility in which we can all share. So dear reader, analyze your relationships and base them around *taqwa*, ponder over the chain reaction, strengthen and guard your *taqwa* using the checklist and play a crucial part in saving the souls of people from the deliberately created deception that is all around us.

If you want to know where you need to get to, then let none other than Abu Bakr As Siddiq, *radiya'llahu 'anhu*, lead the way:

Abu Bakr, *radiya'llahu 'anhu*, used to have a servant-boy who would collect the *kharaj* (a tax paid by non-Muslims in return for protection from the Islamic state) for him, and Abu Bakr, *radiya'llahu 'anhu*, would buy food for himself out of this money. One day, however, the boy brought something, and Abu Bakr, *radiya'llahu 'anhu*, ate it. 'Do you know what that was?' the boy asked, and Abu Bakr, *radiya'llahu 'anhu*, said, 'What?' 'In the *jahiliyya* (period of ignorance)," he said, 'I was a soothsayer; something which, in fact, I did not know how to do, but I deceived a man, who met me just now and gave me what you ate.' And Abu Bakr, *radiya'llahu 'anhu*, put his finger into his throat and vomited all that was in his stomach." (Bukhari)

THE HOLY QUR'AN

ABU AZ-ZAHIRIYYAH NARRATED: "I WENT to Tarsus, so I entered upon Abu Mu'awiyah al-Aswad after he had become blind. In his house, I saw a mushaf (copy of the Qur'an)hanging from the wall, so I said to him: 'May Allah have mercy upon you! A mushaf while you cannot even see?'

"He replied: 'My brother, will you keep a secret for me until the day I die?'

"I said: 'Yes.' Then, he said to me: 'Verily, when I want to read from the Qur'an, my eyesight comes back to me.'" (Dhahabi's Siyar A'lam an-Nubala)

Ask yourself the following question:

What does the Qur'an mean to me?

If you have been truthful, and your answer is not much or not as much as you would like it to be, then this chapter will give you some useful tips on how to use the Qur'an in a much more fun and practical way when learning and inviting others to see the greatness of Allah's magnificent book. By the end of the chapter, you should have a useful approach that serves as an inspirational and educational tool.

The beauty of the Qur'an is that it can be used to win people's hearts; it can be what you want it to be, and it can be related to anyone from any walk of life. It carries a seamless and endless reservoir of knowledge and amazingly stands the test of time. It is a book that can bring cures to illnesses, enlighten hearts, inspire, bring tears to the eyes, guide and provide superhuman abilities to those who know how to unlock its power. It is a condensed version of the Divine Tablet that contains all knowledge, thus giving it supremacy over all previous books that contained only part of the knowledge that is found in the Qur'an. While all previous books were only sent to a particular nation, the Qur'an is for everyone, and the proof is in Allah's statement, "Oh mankind" (*Ya ayyuhan Nas*).

The problem we face today lies in the way the Qur'an is being taught. It is no exaggeration to state that the traditional style of teaching children how to read the Qur'an in a parrot fashion is detrimental to showcasing its beauty to the wider world and is hindering the potential for future generations to use it as a tool and instrument for *da'wa*, especially when the *maulvi* (religious teacher) throws in a few kicks and punches when unsuspecting parents are turned the other way. The child should understand the Qur'an's potential from an early age and should be able to relate to it when he comes of age. He can then be in a position to help others relate to it. The Qur'an's exceptional qualities, healing ability, cures of the heart, power and knowledge should be instilled in every Muslim from the outset. Some general trivia may be helpful on things that are less well known about the Qur'an, such as modern commentaries on verses that the child will find fascinating and useful (please note that this takes a certain caliber of scholar and not just the average imam in the local mosque). There is so much in the Qur'an that gives it the "wow" factor that we really have no excuse in this regard, and if we want our children to grow up with a high, personal and meaningful view of the Qur'an, then trivia, general knowledge, amazing facts, science, inspirational commentaries should be taught from the outset as part of the curriculum.

The way the Qur'an has been taught has not evolved, and parents should call for a change in this comfortable arrangement of getting the job of teaching their children the Qur'an over and done with, and the *maulvi* getting the numbers in. For generations, there has been no emphasis on the practical implementation of the Qur'an in the real world. Instead of learning the Qur'an in a parrot fashion way and then trying to understand it in the context of the real world, I think more emphasis should be placed on understanding the world we live in and then applying it to what we know from the Qur'an. In today's material world, we need professionals like doctors, lawyers and engineers with knowledge of the world as well as Islam. So if you are a parent, find out which institutions teach the knowledge of both Islam and *dunya* if you want a well-educated, professional child who is also on the straight path (as opposed to a straight forward traditional *madrasa* (traditional Islamic school)).

Look at what the following verses allude to:

"Do they not look at the Camels, how they are made
And at the Sky, how it is raised high
And at the Mountains, how they are fixed firm
And at the Earth, how it is spread out?"
(Qur'an, 88:17-20)

"In that are Signs indeed for those who reflect."
(Qur'an, 45:13)

The verses are proving my point that we should understand the world. Moreover, we should investigate our surroundings, people and society. In the above verses, Allah is asking us to find out and learn about animals; He is asking us to learn about orography (the study of mountains) and to learn the sciences associated with the earth. This is because we can truly appreciate Allah through His creation, and from a practical *da'wa* standpoint, understanding the Qur'an will be a lot more meaningful if we understand that which affects us and others first. It puts a person in a much stronger position if his or her knowledge of various subjects is coupled with knowledge of the Qur'an, as opposed to having just knowledge of the Qur'an alone.

Allah says:

"And verily We have put forth for mankind in this Qur'an every kind of example, that they may reflect." (Qur'an, 39:27)

The verse illustrates that the Qur'an can have a personal meaning to all of us, since it contains knowledge of everything. In other words, there is something in it for everyone, from any walk of life and background. In essence, martial arts, geology, science, planet formation or whatever subject you aspire to can all be found. For example, martial arts use a combination of kicks and punches, and although the Qur'an does not overtly use a combination of this kind, Allah did, however, say to Ayyub, *alayhi's-salam, "…strike with your foot,"* (Qur'an, 38:41) so that a spring of fresh water could be used to cure him of his illnesses.

This strategy of placing emphasis on learning about the world first will increase the number of people you can speak to about Islam; it will command respect and will allow you to widen your sphere of influence. If you know how engineering relates to the Qur'an, you can speak to engineers; if you know how cosmology relates to the Qur'an, you can speak to people about planet formation from a Qur'anic point of view; if you come across people who believe in nature, you can speak to people about the camel, the bee and the ant from the Qur'an's perspective. Thus, be an expert in the subjects that interest you, find them in the Qur'an and when you come across people who share the same interests, you have a powerful platform from which to work.

On a micro level, there are also other practical ways of using the Qur'an to change people and help them. This is because every verse of the Qur'an is special in its own way. For centuries, people have been using the Qur'an to achieve wonderful and amazing things illustrating that the right guidance, *taqwa* and knowledge can put a person in a position of great power. Even if we can learn the blessings and power of a few of these verses, it can add a lot of value when guiding people towards Islam. According to commentators, it is widely accepted that the complete knowledge of the Holy Qur'an is contained in the *Fatiha* (opening chapter of the Qur'an). All the knowledge in *Fatiha* is contained within the *Basmala* (*Bismillah ir-Rahman ir-Raheem*, in the name of Allah, the Compassionate, the Merciful). All the knowledge in the *Basmala* is contained in the letter "*Ba*." All the knowledge of the letter "*Ba*" is contained in the dot.

Since the first word of the Holy Qur'an is "*Bismillah*," let's take a look at the extraordinary blessing associated with it:

Qays ibn Abî Hâzim said: "I saw poison being brought to Khâlid, and it was asked, 'What is this?' The answer was given, 'It is poison.' He said, 'Bismillâh,' and drank it. I said, 'By Allâh, this is a miracle; this is true courage.'"

Abu's-Safar said: "Khâlid stayed in al-Hîrah at the house of the mother of the Banû Marâzibah. They said, 'Be on your guard against the Persians, lest they poison you.' He said, 'Bring it to me.' He took it and said, '*Bismillâh*,' and it did him no harm. (Dhahabi's Siyar A'lam an-Nubala)

Ahmad bin Fudayl narrated:

"Abu Mu'awiyah al-Aswad went out and took part in a battle in which the Muslims had surrounded a fortress on top of which a '*ilj* (Roman disbeliever) was standing who would not throw an arrow or a stone except that he would strike his target. The Muslims complained about this to Abu Mu'awiyah, so he recited: (*'And it was not you who threw when you threw. Rather, it was Allah who threw...'*) (Qur'an, 8: 17)

Then, he said: 'Shield me from him.'

"Then he got up and said: 'Where do you wish for me to strike him?'

"They said: 'In his private parts.'

"Abu Mu'awiyah said: 'O Allah! You have heard what they have asked of me, so grant me what they ask of me!' Then he said, '*Bismillah*,' and shot the arrow.

The arrow went straight for the wall of the fortress, seemingly about to miss the disbeliever. Then, right when it was about to hit the wall, it changed course and shot straight up, striking the '*ilj* in his private parts.

"Abu Mu'awiyah then said: 'Your problem with him is over.'" (Dhahabi's Siyar A'lam an-Nubala)

On the blessings of the first *Ayat*, *Surah Fatiha*:

Narrated Ibn 'Abbas:

"Some of the companions of the Prophet passed by some people staying at a place where there was water, and one of them had been stung by a scorpion. A man from those staying near the water came and said to the companions of the Prophet, 'Is there anyone among you who can do ruqya (spiritual healing) as near the water there is a person who has been stung by a scorpion.' So one of the Prophet's companions went to him and recited Surat-al-Fatiha for a sheep as his fees. The patient was cured, and the man brought the sheep to his companions who disliked that and said, 'You have taken wages for reciting Allah's Book.' When they arrived at Medina, they said, 'O Allah's Apostle! (This person) has taken wages for reciting Allah's Book.' On that Allah's Apostle said, 'You are most entitled to take wages for doing a ruqya with Allah's Book.'" (Bukhari.

There is another narration similar to this in Bukhari).

In conclusion, I have presented an approach that makes us knowledgeable in our surroundings first. This knowledge should then be applied to and extracted from the Qur'an to place us in a much more favorable stance in front of the wider world. As for, the qualities of each verse, my advice is for you is to learn the qualities of some of the verses of the Qur'an and then add them to the tools already at your disposal. This should be done by seeking out a certain type of scholar who has this particular knowledge of the Qur'an. The same scholar should also be able to guide you to how you can find knowledge of your subjects of interest from the Qur'an.

Part Two

Techniques and New Age Concepts for Better Results

Winning Hearts and Minds

WHEN SOMEONE DOES GOOD TO YOU, you are happy, and when you do good to someone, they are happy. In that, there is a great opening. I once asked a great shaykh, "What is the best way to guide someone?" He replied, "Guide people how they want to be guided."

Oh reader, every person loves someone or something; find it, and use what they love to win their hearts.

"None of you can truly be said to believe until he loves for his brother what he loves for himself." (Bukhari)

I'm sure the *mujtahid* imams (Muslim scholar qualified to carry out *ijtihad* (the exercise of personal judgment in legal matters)), who are two a penny nowadays will have something to say about my use of spin here! I know that the *hadith* has been interpreted to mean "brothers in humanity and wanting Islam for them," but I believe that there are hidden layers to every *hadith* and verse in the Qur'an, and the above *hadith* is no exception to this.

Speak to people how you would like to be spoken to, listen to them how you would like to be listened to, act with them in the manner how you would like them to act towards you, treat them how you would like to be treated in every respect, and you have found a way to winning their hearts and minds. Furthermore, show empathy towards their likings, such as their family members, their community, their culture, and their belongings that they hold dear, and you have the secret to their hearts.

So, dear readers, what is the key to winning a heart and mind?

In 2003, the American military launched an operation to invade Iraq under the doctrine called "Shock and Awe." The idea behind the doctrine was simply to use overwhelming force to leave the enemy in complete shock and to leave them completely debilitated. After two weeks of lighting up the Baghdad skyline, the U.S. administration began to implement a strategy of winning hearts and minds. The problem was, after annihilating everything in existence and killing everything in sight and that which was not in sight, it proved very difficult to then convince a person that despite killing his whole family, wiping out his entire generation, completely destroying his livelihood, and watching everything he built vanish into oblivion, that the Americans meant well! The net result of the "hearts and minds" campaign was an insurgency that wanted to pay back the nice American gesture.

On the subject of winning hearts and minds, the Prophet, *sall-Allahu alayhi wa sallam*, was already using the concept of "Shock and Awe" but in a much nicer and more effective manner. It was the "Shock and Awe" of the heart by repaying evil with good. This concept was used by later *shuyukh* (leaders, plural of shaykh) to great effect. The idea was that, if someone did something evil to you and you repaid them with good, the response would be so overwhelming to the heart that it would leave the person no choice but to be left in complete awe and admiration. Coupled with the fact that the person delivering the shock was a Muslim would leave the other person with no choice but to accept the religion.

It is well known that Abu Hanifa, may God have mercy on his soul, used to perform the *tahajjud* prayer every night. He would spend his night reciting the Qur'an. He had a neighbor who was an alcoholic, and the neighbor used to drink a lot and sing love poems. This used to bother the imam

However, one day, the *imam* did not hear this man's revelry, so he went and asked about him. They said, "Oh, so-and-so. They took him to jail." So, the very well respected *imam* went to the jail. He was the most respected *imam* and *qadi* (a Muslim religious judge) at the time in that place. When the ruler found out the imam went to the jail, he asked for the reason and was told that the *imam* was concerned about his neighbor who had been arrested. So, the ruler said to release the man, and he was released.

The neighbor then asked Abu Hanifa why he did that, and he replied, "Because you have a right upon me as a neighbor, and I have not been neglectful of that." Upon hearing Abu hanifa's response the neighbor made *tawba* (turning to Allah, asking for His forgiveness, and turning away from error) to Allah, *subhânahu wa ta'âla* (glorfied and exalted is He).

So dear reader, why not launch your own campaign of winning hearts and minds using "Shock and Awe." You could even have some fun in the process by giving each potential target an operation name, but instead of physical harm, you would be applying spiritual awe in the hearts and minds of whoever behaves badly towards you. Before you know it, you'd have successful sorties and successful campaigns, all of which would be winning you new friends, helping you to follow a tremendously powerful *sunnah*, earning the great pleasure of Allah, and giving yourself a great sense of personal achievement.

On top of "Shock and Awe," psychologically speaking, profiling people for each campaign can greatly increase your chances of success. This is because people can be split into various category types, and this knowledge can be very useful in deciding what approach you need to take in winning a person's heart and mind. The categories can be broken down as follows:

- Towards people
- Away people
- Optional people
- Procedural people

Towards people are those who usually react positively to what they may gain if they undertake a certain decision or action. They are usually open to suggestions, positive people, outgoing and results driven. They are often used to taking decisions.

Away people are cautious and usually take decisions based on what they may lose if they do not undertake a decision or action. They are usually negative, hands off and conservative.

Optional people like options and react positively if they have more than one option, whereas procedural people do not react well to options but do to procedures. Doctors are procedural people for example.

The beauty of knowing which category a person falls under is that Islam offers something for each category. Hope and fear are concepts often spoken about but never truly implemented in the correct way, and understanding how a person reacts can place us in a powerful position. So when we know someone is a "towards" person, we can use hope, and when we know a person falls under the "away" category, we can use "fear." Furthermore, when a person is more akin to procedures, we can stress upon what steps can be taken in Islam for him to achieve the results he wants, and when a person is more akin to options, we can give him the choices of how he can achieve what he wants.

THE POWER OF POSITIVE THOUGHTS IN ISLAM

TAKE A GLASS; FILL IT WITH water half way. Now ask yourself, "Is it half empty or half full?"

The power of thought is underrated. Changing thoughts can alter a lot more than what we think, even impacting huge geographical areas and people, even changing generations to come, as we will see in this section. Although we can only think about what we know, thoughts are not spatially confined, and we can think about things in any manner and how we like. They can take us on a downward spiral with no floor or raise us upwards towards a place with no ceiling. Look at manic-depressives who have hit rock bottom, and look at enthusiasts with the sky as their limit. Thus, if we apply this to da'wa, negativity and positivity will be detected either consciously or subconsciously by whomever you come into contact with, and this will either help or hinder you in giving them *da'wa*. However, please note that knowing which tools to use in which situation will require judgment. Therefore if you are being overtly positive and not applying empathy to a person who is suicidal and he then jumps out of the window, don't scratch your head in bemusement!

Positive thinking can also provide an opening for influence when dealing with adversaries. It is so powerful that when positive thought is used in a good way, no adversary, no situation can harm you. Dealing with enemies to overcome them and bring them "on side" is a great way to affect change in them eventually.

I had a manager at work who asked me, "So are you a fundamentalist or a moderate?" I replied, "In Islam, we either follow the rules or break them." I wondered why he asked me this question, and after some days of him passing some comments and him trying to wind me up, it finally dawned on me. He wanted to prove his own belief that all Muslims were extremists. So the question remained, would I allow him to prove his theory right and finally explode under the taunts and pressure, or would I find a strategy to change the momentum and shift the situation to my advantage where I was the one calling the shots and using his negativity against him. Thus, I decided that I would use the *sunnah* of positive thinking to calm myself down and change the stakes. I then thought of the greatest reasons why I should respect this man. It was simple. He was instrumental and paramount in my learning curve that would help me establish my career, and he was fundamentally important in helping me earn my living. These two things were enough for me to give him the respect that would not allow me to confront him. In my mind, these two things alone outweighed all the flaws I could find in him. The result of my strategy showed me firsthand the benefits of thinking positively because over time my manager became more comfortable with me. I didn't react in a way where his negative views on Islam became further entrenched, and I also had openings to show him the beauty of Islam. All this came from positive thinking.

After all isn't this what Hazrat Umar, *radiya'llahu 'anhu,* used when a man came to see him to complain about his wife? When the man approached the house of Hazrat Umar, *radiya'llahu 'anhu,* he could hear that Umar's wife was shouting and being abusive to him. The man left, but Hazrat Umar, *radiya'llahu 'anhu,* saw him and caught up with him. When the man explained why he had come and saw that Hazrat Umar, *radiya'llahu 'anhu,* was being spoken to in this way, he asked why he did not say anything to her. Hazrat Umar, *radiya'llahu 'anhu,* said, "Is it not true that she prepares food for me, washes clothes for me and suckles my children, thus saving me the expense of employing a cook, a washer man and a nurse, though she is not legally obliged in any way to do any of these things? Besides, I enjoy peace of mind because of her and am kept away from indecent acts on account of her. I, therefore, tolerate all her excesses because of these benefits. It is right that you should also adopt the same attitude."

Even those among us who seek knowledge, if we apply positive and negative thoughts to the Qur'an and *hadith*, you will be surprised to see two different types of *tafseer* (commentary and explanation of meaning).

Look at this hadith below:

Abu Hurairah, *radiya'llahu 'anhu,* reported that the Prophet, *sall-Allahu alayhi wa sallam,* said, *"Whoever sends salutations on me, Allah returns my soul to my body, and I reply to his salaam."* (Abu Dawood).

The negative way to look at this is to limit the position of the Prophet, *sall-Allahu alayhi wa sallam,* and to focus on his dependence on Allah to do anything. Of course, it goes without saying that we are all subject to the will of Allah.

The positive way to look at the hadith is to see the freedom the Prophet, *sall-Allahu alayhi wa sallam,* has to travel wherever he likes. Since hundreds, thousands, even millions of people may be reciting salutations upon the Prophet around the world at the same time (take the congregational *jumma'a* prayer in any one country for example), it is proof of the extraordinary position and ability of the Prophet, *sall-Allahu alayhi wa sallam,* that he is replying to each person simultaneously, be it one, two, a hundred, or even millions of people. Superman, Neo, Harry Potter, eat your hearts out!

Now look at this hadith:

"He who invokes blessings upon me by my grave, I will hear him, and he who invokes blessings upon me from a distance, it will be conveyed to me." (Baihaqi)

The negative way to look at this is to see that the Prophet is limited in his hearing from the grave. However, read the *hadith* again, and the positive among us will be able to see that the Prophet is not at all saying he is unable to hear us from a distance. He's just not admitting it openly. The Qur'an shows us that in fact the Prophet is able to know what we are doing from anywhere since Allah says, *"The Prophet is closer to the believers than their own selves"* (Qur'an, Surah 33:6). The word for "*selves*" used by Allah is "*anfusihim*," which is derived from the root word "*nafs*." (To illustrate how close the Prophet, *sall-Allahu alayhi wa sallam*, is to us, if our *nafs* is removed from our bodies, we will die). Thus, Allah is telling us that the Prophet, *sall-Allahu alayhi wa sallam*, knows everything about us, including what we are saying and doing, and in fact does not need to have an intermediary at all to convey blessings to him.

On the subject of positive thinking, there has been a lot of focus on a particular law that is being sold as the ticket to everyone's material dreams. That law is the "Law of Attraction." This law promises great wealth and material gain through positive thinking. Indeed, the very idea of a material heaven on earth should raise the question of whom is this law serving in the first place? The devil, maybe? Well, for those of us who haven't come across this law, it's a simple theory stating that through either positive or negative thoughts, we are responsible for everything that we have attracted in our lives. Thus, if we are poor, it is our mindset that is attracting poverty and keeping us in it. For example, instead of thinking, "I don't want to be broke anymore," we should change our thought process to, "I want to be rich." According to adherents to this law, four things are required:

1. Know exactly what you want.
2. Ask the universe for it.
3. Feel, behave, and know as if the object of your desire is already yours (visualize).
4. Be open to receive it, and let go of (the attachment to) the outcome.

Notice the second point. Here's lies a very powerful clue as to whom the law is serving. It's almost as if the devil is doing a tradeoff here. I'll tell you how to be wealthy and successful through a hidden law, but in return just replace God with the universe. The flaw, however, is that the universe is itself a created thing and cannot give or take anything from its own doing. It is itself subject to billions of laws that are all created themselves.

But saying this, is the law of attraction completely false, and can it be found in Islamic scripture? Does the Qur'an say anything on this subject?

"If anything good happens, it is from Allah; if anything bad happens, it is from your own selves." (Qur'an, 4:79)

This verse is telling us that if you have attracted something bad, then it is your own fault. In other words, you have attracted it through your actions. Now, you may be thinking that this verse is speaking about actions only and not thoughts, but aren't thoughts precursors to actions? Thus, a positive or negative thought process translates into a positive or negative action.

Look at this verse: *"If you are grateful, I will surely increase you."* (Qur'an, 14:7)

Gratitude leads to an increase, and gratitude is undoubtedly a positive thing in itself. This is further proof that positive thoughts can lead to accumulation of whatever we desire if Allah wills. It is confirming that we have the power to attract things via positive thoughts and is another confirmation of the Law of Attraction.

An amazing example of the above verse and how positive thinking can increase you is the story of Taif. This is a beautiful story of compassion, humility, patience, and most of all positivity. It is a real life example of the Law of Attraction.

Bukhari and Muslim both record the story as narrated by Hazrat Aisha, *radiya'llahu 'anha.* In this incident, the Prophet, *sall-Allahu alayhi wa sallam*, was ridiculed and stoned by the people of Taif who would not accept his call to Islam. The stoning was severe, drawing blood, and particularly humiliating as it was at the hands of young children. The

Prophet, *sall-Allahu alayhi wa sallam,* was then visited by Jibril and an angel who was in charge of the mountains, and he was given the choice of destroying the inhabitants of the Taif. However, the Prophet replied with a *dua* preferring to see future generations of Muslims from the same people who had stoned him. Soon after this *dua*, the people of Taif embraced Islam and are Muslim to this day.

So, if we look at this with the Law of Attraction in mind, the negative was changed into a positive thought and action, and its effects are being felt 1400 years later. How many Muslims will be standing in the party of the Holy Prophet, *sall-Allahu alayhi wa sallam*, on the Day of Judgment from this one incident alone? The Prophet, *sall-Allahu alayhi wa sallam,* was grateful; he was positive in his thinking, and Allah increased him because of it. Just look at what one positive thought did for the Prophet, *sall-Allahu alayhi wa sallam*, for Islam, and for the *ummah*? One thought, one *dua* = millions of followers.

Imam Ahmed in his Musnad records a narration where a Bedouin came to the Prophet, *sall-Allahu alayhi wa sallam*, and asked him a number of questions. One of the questions was about wealth. He asked, "I want to be the richest man in the world." The Prophet replied, "Be happy with what you have, and you will be the richest man in the world." In other words, be grateful, and you will be increased. Those who know about the Law of Attraction also know that being content and giving thanks for what you have is a major part in accumulating more.

So readers, if you want to change others around you and want to accumulate more of whatever it is you desire, start thinking positively. Be grateful, and remember that your thoughts can have a big impact on what you want to achieve. If you want to adopt the Islamic version of the Law of Attraction, then follow the above four steps, replacing the universe with Allah.

Since *da'wa* is a numbers game, you can set a target in your mind of how many people you want to influence, visualise achieving the target, act as though you have achieved it and visualize the steps that need to be taken in order to achieve it. Start with "*Bismillah*," and end with "*Alhumdulillah*."

Now look at the same glass of water, is it still half empty?

Ingroups and Outgroups in Islam

EVER WONDERED WHY YOUR SPHERE OF influence is so small?Ever wanted to know the secret of reverting others? The concept of "ingroups" and "outgroups" holds the key.

The concept of ingroups and outgroups has been with us throughout time. It has been the single biggest factor in starting wars, creating divisions, and contributing to various injustices on different levels. The concept in its simplest form is that all humans gravitate towards other humans who share common characteristics. Thus, if I am brown and you are brown, you automatically form part of my ingroup. If you are from my hometown, again you are part of my ingroup and vice versa. Although ingroups can be harmless, such as if the other person supports the same football club, very often, however, we tend to categorize our ingroups according to far more prejudicial criteria, such as race, ethnicity, religion, nationality, gender, etc.

"O mankind! We created you from a single (pair) of a male and a female and made you into nations and tribes that ye may know each other." (Qur'an, 49:13)

This verse tells us that our differences are not for us to find a reason to separate and form ingroups and outgroups. It is a reason to embrace change and difference, and this is the beauty of life. If everything were the same, it would get boring. Our beauty lies in our differences, whether that means color, ethnicity, nationality, etc.

Thus, if we want to have an impact on others, we must accept differences and blur the lines that exclude people from our ingroup. *We must make all the normal considerations that make us usually place a person in our outgroup unimportant so that eventually they become our ingroup.*

The larger the ingroup gets, the greater the sphere of influence.

So next time you meet a new person, don't allow your instincts to take over on the normal grounds that usually allow you to classify them as belonging to your inner circle or to your outgroup. Remember this, and hit the override button! We always speak about networking from a business point of view; why shouldn't we have a method for effective Islamic networking for da'wa purposes?

The Prophet, *sall-Allahu alayhi wa sallam,* was the most effective networker in the history of mankind because he knew that these boundaries that would have placed others in his outgroup would be prejudicial and contrary to his call towards Islam. After all, he embraced the young and the old, the weak and the strong, the oppressed and the free, the rich and the poor, women and men, the fair skinned and the dark skinned. In other words, he only had an ingroup, and everything else was secondary.

Look at how the Qur'an speaks about this concept, the concept of one ingroup:

"We did not send you except as a mercy to the universe." (Qur'an, 21:107)

Then there is the following *hadith*, which further proves the concept:

Jabir narrated that the Prophet said: "I have been given five things which no prophet was given before me:

"1. Allah made me victorious by awe (by His frightening my enemies) for a distance of one month's journey.

"2. The earth has been made for me (and for my followers) a place for praying and a thing to perform *tayammum* (ritual ablution using dust or the earth when water is unavailable). Therefore, my followers can pray wherever the time of a prayer is due.

"3. The booty has been made *halal* (lawful) for me (and was not made so for anyone else).

"4. *Every Prophet used to be sent to his nation exclusively, but I have been sent to all mankind.*

"5. I have been given the right of intercession (on the Day of Resurrection.)." (Bukhari)

The Prophet, *sall-Allahu alayhi wa sallam*, had the biggest ingroup in history and the biggest sphere of influence. His ingroup to date consists of approximately 1.5 billion people. Who can boast of a larger ingroup than that?

Before the name Jesus, *'alayhi's-salam*, comes to mind, consider the following points carefully:

1. Jesus, *'alayhi's-salam,* was sent to Bani Israel only

2. He will return as a follower of he Prophet Muhammad and will implement Islamic *Shariah* rather than his own.

3. The majority who claim to follow him are not following his original message at all, since he was not a Trinitarian.

ALLAH'S USE OF NEURO LINGUISTIC PROGRAMMING (NLP)

Someone I know was worried about not having a large enough circle of friends, so he made a *dua* asking Allah to make him more likeable. A week later he sat down with someone in his company who introduced him to Neuro Linguistic Programming. He was astonished to see how effective the concept was when practiced and how it didn't conflict with his belief in Islam.

Most of us have heard the saying, "People buy people," but how many of us actually know how to make people buy into us without them even knowing it. NLP helps us understand how people think and act and is a very effective way of influencing individuals and even large groups of people.

Those of us who don't know what NLP is, it explores the relationships between how we think (neuro), how we communicate (linguistic) and our patterns of behavior and emotion (programmes).

Or another way to look at it is:

"Neuro" refers to our nervous system, including the brain and the five senses.

"Linguistic" refers to verbal and non-verbal languages with which we communicate.

"Programming" refers to the ability to structure our neurological and linguistic systems to achieve desired results.

Within NLP, there are a number of models that allow people to obtain various results, helping them to stimulate change within themselves, as well as stimulating change in others.

The model that is often cited as the most effective in influencing people is known as "Representational Systems." This system focuses on hearing, sight, and feelings and says that we process information and make decisions using our senses. Thus, one talks to oneself (the auditory sense), even if no words are emitted. One makes pictures in one's head when thinking or dreaming (the visual sense), and one considers feelings in the body and emotions (known as the kinesthetic sense). Different people respond to situations according to one, two or all three of the senses stated. How many times have we heard the following expressions?

"I hear you"- Auditory

"I see what you mean"- Visual

"I feel you"- Kinesthetic

Very often, the key to finding out who is what, depends on a person's job and how they have been trained. Very often what they do for a living is a give away. (Getting through to an accountant, for example, will need the visual modality, and using only speech will not be enough).

For *da'wa* purposes, guiding or helping someone can be a lot easier if we know how people respond. Some people may need to see evidences. Some people may go by how their heart responds and some by only hearing evidences. If we know which type of category they fit into, we can have a much bigger impact on them.

In the 12th and 13th centuries, the *Chisti Sufi* order was instrumental in reverting millions of Hindus in India, and the way they did it was simple. NLP played an instrumental role.

Since Hindus were fond of music, the *shaykh* (leader) of this *Sufi* order used *qawwali* (Sufi singing in Urdu or Persian) to amazing effect. Since *qawwali* induced ecstatic states (kinesthetic), whoever listened (auditory) to them automatically fell in love. The stage was thus set for giving and receiving spiritual help. (Please see the treatise on music and its effects by Imam Ghazali in Ihya Ulum Ud Din.)

The Prophet, *sall-Allahu alayhi wa sallam*, used NLP on numerous occasions.

Tirmidhi records a narration where the Prophet, *sall-Allahu alayhi wa sallam,* was giving advice to someone, saying, "Beware of this," and he grabbed his tongue. "I and the one who takes care of the orphans are in Paradise, like this." The Prophet, *sall-Allahu alayhi wa sallam*, then joined his two fingers together. (Bukhari)

Ahmad records a *hadith* where the Prophet, *sall-Allahu alayhi wa sallam*, drew four lines in the sand and said, "Do you know what these are?" They said, "Allah and His Messenger know best." So he, *sall-Allahu alayhi wa sallam*, said: "These are the best of women in Jannah: Khadijah bint Khuwaalid, Fatimah bint Muhammad, Maryam bint Imraan, and Asiya bint Mazahim (the wife of Pharaoh)."

In fact, the instances where the Prophet, *sall-Allahu alayhi wa sallam*, used diagrams to illustrate certain points have been recorded by numerous people, including Al Hakim, Ahmad, Ibn Majah, and Bazzar.

The use of diagrams, hand gestures, and even kinesthetic (feelings) are all *sunnah*. The instances of people accepting Islam on feelings alone are numerous, such as the lady who would throw rubbish over the Prophet daily. When she was not seen by the Prophet, *sall-Allahu alayhi wa sallam*, he enquired about her well-being. He was informed that she was unwell. Upon his visiting her, she was so touched by this that she accepted Islam.

Hazrat Umar, *radiya'llahu 'anhu,* accepted Islam after reading some verses of Qur'an. (Could it be that he was responsive to visual more than anything else?)

Since the heading of the chapter is about Allah 's use of NLP, let me finish by proving that NLP is nothing new and that we are in many respects quite primitive in our understanding, intellect and knowledge. What is the Qur'an if it isn't a visual and auditory aid? It is coupled with a living example in the Prophet, *sall-Allahu alayhi wa sallam*, who inspired and aroused the truth to become manifest in us. We are, in the end, being guided in a visual, auditory and kinesthetic way even today.

Risk Management

"Fear God wherever you are; let an evil deed (be) followed by a good deed so that you blot it out, and be well-behaved towards people." (Ahmad, Tirmidhi)

I once had the pleasure of sitting with the director of marketing for Shell on a flight to the UK. During a conversation on marketing techniques, she made a point that has stayed with me until today. She told me that every person has a risk, and if you can successfully identify that risk and manage it, he or she will become your client.

Although, the point is a prudent one for promoting a service, a business, or anything commercially related, it is in fact something that can be easily applied to *da'wa*, and the concept itself has its roots firmly based in Islam. Allah says, *"Take care of yourselves: If you follow (right) guidance, no hurt can come to you from those who stray. The goal of you all is to Allah. It is He that will show you the truth of all that you do."* (Qur'an, Surah 5:105) Here, Allah is making a direct reference to risk mitigation from and management of enemies, and He is even telling us how to manage it through sticking to guidance and remembering the Day of Judgment.

Furthermore, look at the Final Sermon of the Prophet, *sall-Allahu alayhi wa sallam:*

"O people, lend me an attentive ear, for I know not whether after this year, I shall ever be amongst you again. Therefore, listen to what I am saying to you very carefully, and take these words to those who could not be present here today.

"O people, just as you regard this month, this day, this city as sacred, so regard the life and property of every Muslim as a sacred trust. Return the goods entrusted to you to their rightful owners. Hurt no

one, so that no one may hurt you. Remember that you will indeed meet your Lord and that He will indeed reckon your deeds. Allah has forbidden you to take usury (interest). Therefore, all interest obligation shall henceforth be waived. Your capital, however, is yours to keep. You will neither inflict nor suffer any inequity. Allah has judged that there shall be no interest and that all the interest due to Abbas ibn 'Abd al Muttalib (the Prophet's uncle) shall henceforth be waived…

"Beware of Satan, for the safety of your religion. He has lost all hope that he will ever be able to lead you astray in big things, so beware of following him in small things.

"O people, it is true that you have certain rights with regard to your women, but they also have rights over you. Remember that you have taken them as your wives only under Allah's trust and with His permission. If they abide by your right, then to them belongs the right to be fed and clothed in kindness. Do treat your women well, and be kind to them for they are your partners and committed helpers. And it is your right that they do not make friends with anyone of whom you do not approve, as well as never to be unchaste.

"O people, listen to me in earnest, worship Allah, say your five daily prayers (salah), fast during the month of Ramadan, and give your wealth in zakat. Perform hajj if you can afford to.

"All mankind is from Adam and Eve. An Arab has no superiority over a non-Arab, nor does a non-Arab have any superiority over an Arab; also a white person has no superiority over a black person, nor does a black person have any superiority over a white person except by piety and good action. Learn that every Muslim is a brother to every Muslim and that the Muslims constitute one brotherhood. Nothing shall be legitimate to a Muslim that belongs to a fellow

Muslim unless it was given freely and willingly. Do not, therefore, do injustice to yourselves.

"Remember, one day you will appear before Allah and answer for your deeds. So beware; do not stray from the path of righteousness after I am gone.

"O people, no prophet or apostle will come after me, and no new faith will be born. Reason well, therefore, O people, and understand the words that I convey to you. I leave behind me two things, the Qu'ran and my example, the sunnah, and if you follow these, you will never go astray.

"All those who listen to me shall pass on my words to others and those to others again, and may the last ones understand my words better than those who listen to me directly. Be my witness, O Allah, that I have conveyed your message to your people." (Bukhari)

On a macro level, in this sermon every key threat/risk to a secure place in Paradise is mentioned. There are numerous warnings and risks that can be extrapolated into the categories listed below. How amazing that the Final Sermon should contain every important aspect of a Muslim's life:

1. Character (Hurt no one, so that no one may hurt you)
2. Trade (Allah has forbidden you to take usury; therefore, all interest obligation shall henceforth be waived)
3. *Shaitan* (Beware of Satan)
4. Marriage (O people, it is true that you have certain rights with regard to your women, but they also have rights over you)
5. The five pillars of Islam
6. Unity (Learn that every Muslim is a brother to every Muslim and that the Muslims constitute one brotherhood)
7. The Day of Judgment

8. The straight path (I leave behind me two things, the Qur'an and my example, the *sunnah*)

The safe transition of a person from this world to the next depends on each one of these risks and threats being managed effectively. Our *iman*, our Islam, and our eternal abode will be determined by the above factors.

On the subject of risk from a micro perspective, the Prophet, *sall-Allahu alayhi wa sallam,* gave different advice to different people, and if you look at the advice he gave, it was exactly according to the main risks that were related to that particular person.

On one occasion, a man came to the Messenger of Allah, *sall-Allahu alayhi wa sallam,* and said, "Messenger of Allah, teach me some words by which I can live. Do not make them too much for me, lest I forget." The Messenger of Allah, *sall-Allahu alayhi wa sallam,* said, *"Do not be angry."* (Abu Daood, Bukhari has a similar narration). The scholars have said that this advice was given to the man purely because he had an issue with his anger.

Sufyan b. Abdullah, *radiya'llahu 'anhu,* relates: "I said: 'O Rasulullah (Messenger of Allah), *sall-Allahu alayhi wa sallam,* tell me something that I should adhere to.' Rasulullah, *sall-Allahu alayhi wa sallam,* said: 'Say: 'My Lord is Allah,' then remain steadfast (istiqamah).' I said : 'O Rasulullah, *sall-Allahu alayhi wa sallam,* what do you fear most for me?' *Thereupon Rasulullah, sall-Allahu alayhi wa sallam, took hold of his own tongue and said: 'This.'"* (Tirmidhi)

These are real life instances of risk management by the Prophet, *sall-Allahu alayhi wa sallam.*

When it comes to *da'wa,* a person's risks can vary greatly and can range from material risks to spiritual risks. You may identify them through various means. Once you have the need/risk identified, if you make it your personal quest to help that person manage it, you could have a friend for life who is ready to receive guidance. If you can't help the person directly, then find a person who can. An example is getting someone a job through a person you know, giving someone advice on a problem that you had yourself and solved or on spiritual matters, getting them in front of a qualified *shaykh* with expertise on issues that are related to the person's problems.

After all, if you can get to the root problem that a person faces and you can offer them help, you'll obtain their friendship, trust, and loyalty, and they'll be ready to receive as much guidance as you want to give them.

Sometimes risks can translate into concerns about Islam in the form of questions that nobody has been able to address effectively. Very often, these are difficult but pertinent questions to which the person does not have answers, and they may be hindering his or her acceptance of the religion. Take, for example, the issue of women's rights and the wearing of *hijab*. Look at the "fear syndrome" associated with the word *shariah* (the Islamic legal modality). Look at the issue of the beard. These are all concerns that some people have about personal changes that have to be made. I remember a person telling me once that he loved everything about Islam, except that he could not give up women and alcohol.

The easiest way to deal with such a scenario is to wait until you understand what the person's concerns are. After that, you can either address them yourself if you feel you have the expertise, the wisdom, and the knowledge to deal with the issues, or you can ask someone who you feel can provide comprehensive answers on your behalf. Please be aware that you may only have one shot at this, as your first attempt will leave an imprint and an impression that could prove hard to undo later. So make sure you get it right!

Everyone has a risk, and it may vary. It could be a situation, a personal crisis, a financial need, an addiction, a dispute, stress, loneliness, ill health, black magic, marital problems, children's issues, studies, or even simple questions and concerns about Islam itself, which if you can answer can be an opening for exerting influence.

From a practical point of view, if you like, you can use a model for identifying problems that are relevant to the person you wish to help. The model is taken from the Final Sermon of the Prophet, *sall-Allahu alayhi wa sallam,* and is a macro assessment of risks that a person faces in the most important aspects of Islamic life.

The way to use it is simple. Look at each of the categories mentioned above under the Final Sermon, then apply them one by one to the person you wish to help. Identify the key problems that the person has in each category, and you will obtain a comprehensive snapshot of all the risks the person faces. After that, you are ready to decide what method of help you want to propose. Take it as an information gathering model to identify key risks with a view to providing help and ultimately influence.

The prospect is a married male in his late twenties with two children.

Character – (What are his vices, e.g., zinnah (unlawful sex, either adultery or fornication, consuming alcohol, anger issues, drug addiction.)

Problem with drug addiction

Trade – (What does he or she do for a living? Is it halal or haraam (forbidden)?)

Works as an engineer

Shaitan – (Is there evidence or history of black magic?).

None

Marriage – (Are there problems at home with his marriage and children?)

Anger issues, poor relationships at home, marital issues

The five pillars of Islam – (Does he pray?).

Only prays jumma'a

Unity – (Is there a dysfunctional family? What are his/her friends like?)

Bad circle of friends

The Day of Judgment – (How much taqwa does he have? How is his love for Islam?)

Some signs of love for Islam

The straight path – knowledge and understanding of Islam (Some people may need answers to questions that are causing them confusion, and if you can help them with these questions, it may give them inner peace of heart and mind.)

Does not possess much knowledge of Islam and has certain doubts

From a micro point of view, identify the biggest and the most pressing problems that require urgent attention. Obtaining help on serious and pressing problems will go a long way in winning a person over for life. From my own personal experience, it appears that helping someone deal with some of the most serious problems he faces often leads to loyalty that is unbreakable and incomparable.

Finally, I'll end on an inspirational story about the blessings of helping to solve someone's problems from the time of the great *salaf* (the first three generations of Muslims).

Abd Allah ibn al-Mubarak (d. 797 AD) was living in Makkah. One year, having completed the rites of the pilgrimage, he fell asleep and had a dream wherein he saw two angels descend from heaven.

"How many have come this year?" one asked the other.

"Six hundred thousand," the other replied.

"How many have had their pilgrimage accepted?"

"Not one."

This report filled Abd Allah with trembling. "What?" he cried. "All these people have come from the distant ends of the earth, with great pain and weariness from every deep ravine, traversing wide deserts, and all their labor is in vain?"

"There is a cobbler in Damascus call Ali ibn Mowaffaq," said the first angel. "He has not come on the pilgrimage, but his pilgrimage is accepted, and all his sins have been forgiven."

When he heard this, he awoke and resolved to go to Damascus and visit this person. So he went to Damascus and found where Ali ibn Mowaffaq lived. Abd Allah shouted, and a man came out. "What is your name, and what work do you do?" Abd Allah asked. "I am Ali ibn Mowaffaq, a cobbler by trade. What is your name?"

He told him it was Abd Allah ibn al-Mubarak. Ali then uttered a cry and fell into a faint. When he recovered, Abd Allah begged him to tell him his story. Ali said: "For thirty years now, I have longed to make the pilgrimage. I had saved up three hundred and fifty dirhams (silver coins, each of which was about three grams in weight) from my cobbling. This year I resolved to go to Makkah, though my wife became pregnant. One day she smelled food being cooked next door and begged me to fetch her a bit of it. I went and knocked on the neighbor's door and explained the situation. My neighbor burst into tears. 'My children have eaten nothing for three days,' she said. 'Today I saw a donkey lying dead and cut off a piece and cooked it for them. It would not be lawful food for you.' My heart burned within me when I heard her tale. I took out the three hundred and fifty dirhams and gave them to her. 'Spend these on your children,' I said. 'This is my pilgrimage.'"

"The angel spoke truly in my dream," Abd Allah declared, "and the Heavenly King was true in His judgment." (From Attar's *Memorial of the Saints*)

Words and Phrases

***Adab*:** The term refers to Islamic etiquettes and manners such as respect for elders, how to address parents etc.

Alayhi's-salam: Used after the mention of a Prophet and the angel Gabriel meaning peace be upon him.

***Aleen*:** Plural for the four supreme angels, Jibrail, Mikail, Israfil, Israil.

***Al-fitra*:** "The natural way.'"

***Alhumdulillah*:** Praise be to Allah.

***Alim*:** Islamic scholar.

Ba: An Arabic letter of the alphabet equivalent to the letter "b."

Bait-al Maqdis: Jerusalem where the Mosque of Al Aqsa is located.

Basmala: The term given to the opening verse of the Qur'an: "In the name of Allah, the most Beneficent and the most Merciful."

***Bismillah*:** In the name of Allah.

***Chisti Sufi order*:** Sufi order made famous by Moinudin Chisti.

Da'wa: Propagation of Islam through word and action, calling the people to follow the commandments of Allah and the Prophet Muhammad *sall-Allahu alayhi wa sallam.*

DIRHAMS: A type of Arabic currency.

DUA: Supplication to Allah.

DUNYA: This world or worldly things.

FATIHA: The name of the first chapter of the Qur'an.

FIQH: Islamic jurisprudence derived from Qur'an, sunnah, concensus and analogy.

FITNA: A term used for mischief where it is sometimes difficult to distinguish right from wrong.

HADITH: A saying of the Prophet Muhammad, sall-Allahu alayhi wa sallam.

HADITH QUDSI: A hadith where Allah himself is being quoted.

Hajj: One of the pillars of Islam. The pilgrimage to Mecca.

HALAL: That which is lawful in Islam.

HARAM: That which is unlawful in Islam.

HASAN: A grading of hadith that indicates that the hadith in question is good and reliable.

HIJAB: The scarf used by Muslim women to cover their heads.

HIJRA: The Hijra refers to the Prophet's migration from Mecca to Madinah. This journey took place in the twelfth year of his mission (622 C.E.). This is the beginning of the Muslim calendar.

IFRIT: A powerful type of Jinn.

IJTIHAD: The exercise of personal judgment in legal matters.

ILJ: A roman disbeliever.

IMAM: Muslim religious leader; one who leads the congregational prayer.

IMAN: Faith and sometimes used in conjunction with trust in Allah.

JAHILIYYA: Period of ignorance before the coming of Islam.

JINN: A creation of Allah made from smokeless fire.

JUMMA'A: The Friday prayer performed in congregation at the time of *Zohr*.

KAAFIR: A disbeliever in Allah. It is derived from the root word "*Kafara*" which means to hide or cover up the truth.

KHARAJ: A tax paid by non-Muslims in return for protection from the Islamic state.

MADARIS: Plural for "madrasa" which is a traditional Islamic school.

MAULVI: A religious title given to an Islamic scholar; it precedes the person's name.

MUJTAHID: Muslim religious scholar qualified to carry out independent legal reasoning and the exercise of personal judgment in legal matters.

MUSHAF: A copy of the Qur'an.

NAFS: It has two meanings. Firstly, it means the powers of anger and sexual appetite in a human being, and this is the usage mostly found among the people of tassawwuf [sufis], who take nafs as the comprehensive word for all the evil attributes of a person. The second meaning of nafs is the soul.

QAWWALI: Type of religious devotional music and singing used by the 13th century Sufis.

QADI: Islamic judge.

RADIYA'LLAHU 'ANHA: Used for a female Companion of the Prophet Muhammad after the mention of her name meaning may Allah be pleased with her.

RADIYA'LLAHU 'ANHU: Used for a Companion of the Prophet Muhammad after the mention of his name meaning may Allah be pleased with him.

RAK'AT: A unit of prayer.

RAMADAN: The holy month of prescribed fasting for the Muslims. It was during this month that the Qur'anic revelations began.

***RUQYA*:** Spiritual healing using the Qur'an.

SAHIH: A grading of hadith that indicates that the hadith in question is of the highest reliability and is strong, with no doubts in its chain of narrators.

SALL-ALLAHU ALAYHI WA SALLAM: Used for the Prophet Muhammad after the mention of his name meaning peace and blessing of be upon him.

Sajda: Prostration.

SALAAM: The Islamic greeting of peace.

SALAF: The term used for the first three generations of Muslims.

SALAH: The Arabic name for the five daily prayers.

SHARIAH: The Islamic legal modality. The total legal body of Islamic jurisprudence.

SHIRK: To associate partners with Allah and to worship anyone other than him.

SHUYUKH: Islamic guide/teacher/leader well versed in the Islamic sciences. Plural of Shaykh.

SUBHÂNAHU WA TA'ÂLA: Glorfied and exalted is He (referring to Allah).

SUNNAH: A practice of the Prophet Muhammad *sall-Allahu alayhi wa sallam.*

SUNNI: Abbreviated from the term Ahle Sunnah wa' al Jamma'a which is the main group/body of the Muslims.

Surah: Chapter of the Qur'an.

Tafseer: Commentary on the Qur'an.

Tahajjud: The name given to the supplementary night prayer. Not to be confused with the obligatory night prayer of Isha.

Taif: The name of a town in Saudi Arabia.

Taqwa: The root word for taqwa is "wa ' ka' ya" which means to protect. The simplest definition of taqwa is that it is to be God conscious; to be aware of Allah, to be in awe of Him, and to fear Him.

Tassawwuf: The name given to the practice of spirituality and control of the ego within Sufiism.

Tawba: Turning back to Allah after sinning, asking for His forgiveness, and turning away from error.

Tayammum: Ritual ablution using dust or the earth when water is unavailable.

Ulama: The plural for "Alim", which is the Islamic name for a scholar.

Ummah: A term used for a community or a people. It is used in reference to the community of Believers or Muslims.

Zakat: A pillar of Islam. It is an obligatory charity from one's economic surplus and agricultural income.

ZAMZAM: This is a well/spring located within the Masjid al Haram in Mecca, 20 meters east of the Kaaba, the holiest place in Islam. According to Islamic belief, it was a miraculously-generated source of water from Allah.

ZIKR: Remembrance of Allah.

ZINNAH: To have unlawful sex out of wedlock or to commit adultery.